ACOUSTIC
GUITAR
PRIVATE LESSONS

BABY SONGS AND LULLABIES FOR BEGINNING GUITAR

BY PETER PENHALLOW

STRINGLETTER

STRING LETTER PUBLISHING

Publisher: David A. Lusterman

Group Publisher and Editorial Director: Dan Gabel

Editor: Jeffrey Pepper Rodgers

Music Editor and Engraver: Andrew DuBrock

Art Director: Barbara Summer

Production Director: Hugh O'Connor

Cover Photograph: Rory Earnshaw

Author Photograph: Barbara Summer

Contents © 2010 String Letter Publishing

ISBN 978-1-890490-80-5

This book was produced by Stringletter, Inc.

501 Canal Blvd., Suite J, Richmond, CA 94804

(510) 215-0010; Stringletter.com

STRINGLETTER

STRING LETTER PUBLISHING

Audio

The complete set of audio tracks for the musical examples and songs in *Baby Songs and Lullabies for Beginning Guitar* is available for free download at **store.AcousticGuitar.com/BabySongs**. Just add the tracks to your shopping cart and enter the discount code "**BabySongs**" during checkout to activate your *free* download.

INTRODUCTION

In this songbook are 15 of your favorite baby songs and lullabies, arranged for beginning guitar. You'll learn easy versions of both the melody and rhythm parts, so you can play these songs as guitar instrumentals or accompany singing (the complete lyrics are included). The chords, keys, and techniques used are all taught in Book One of *The Acoustic Guitar Method* and are fundamental to countless styles of traditional guitar music.

I learned music by emulating my own mother, who had picked it up from her father. And I had the great fortune of being an accompanist for many years at a preschool music program where parents would accompany their kids and encourage them to sing. I met and worked with many of those kids later and was struck by their poise, confidence, and good pitch and rhythm. Although they had no conscious recollection of their earlier training, surely it helped give them a solid foundation in music. So playing and singing these songs is rewarding not only for you but for the next generation.

One of the beauties of these songs is their simplicity. The tunes "Mockingbird," "Shoo Fly," "Down in the Valley," "The More We Get Together" and "This Old Man" are the easiest, using only two chords each. "Brahms' Lullaby," "If You're Happy and You Know It," "Kookaburra," "Make New Friends," "The Bear Went Over the Mountain," and "Jenny Jenkins" utilize three chords each. The songs "All the Pretty Little Horses," "Golden Slumbers," "My Bonnie Lies Over the Ocean," and "Over in the Meadow" are slightly more complex, using additional chords that enhance the three-chord structure.

As is common with many baby songs and lullabies, many of the songs in this collection (such as "Golden Slumbers" and "Brahms' Lullaby") are in 3/4 or waltz time. The remainder are in 4/4 or common time. The beautiful "All the Pretty Little Horses" stands out as the one song in this collection that is in a minor, or sad, key. All the rest are in a major, or happy, key.

On the audio tracks, you'll find five tracks for each song. First I play the accompaniment pattern, slowly and then up to tempo (playing at the slower tempo is a great way to program the moves, enabling you to gradually come up to speed).

Next, I play the song as an instrumental, again slowly and up to tempo; and finally I do an abbreviated vocal version, playing the rhythm guitar part and singing the first verse. On the instrumental versions, the rhythm guitar is panned to the left and the guitar melody is on the right, so you can adjust the balance on your stereo if you want to isolate the lead or rhythm.

With a little practice, you should soon be entertaining your family and friends with your favorite baby songs and lullabies.

—Peter Penhallow

 Introduction and Tune-Up

MUSIC NOTATION KEY

The music in this book is written in standard notation and tablature. Here's how to read it.

STANDARD NOTATION

Standard notation is written on a five-line staff. Notes are written in alphabetical order from A to G.

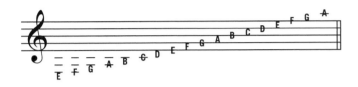

The duration of a note is determined by three things: the note head, stem, and flag. A whole note (𝅝) equals four beats. A half note (𝅗𝅥) is half of that: two beats. A quarter note (♩) equals one beat, an eighth note (♪) equals half of one beat, and a 16th note (𝅘𝅥𝅯) is a quarter beat (there are four 16th notes per beat).

The fraction (4/4, 3/4, 6/8, etc.) or ¢ character shown at the beginning of a piece of music denotes the time signature. The top number tells you how many beats are in each measure, and the bottom number indicates the rhythmic value of each beat (4 equals a quarter note, 8 equals an eighth note, 16 equals a 16th note, and 2 equals a half note). The most common time signature is 4/4, which signifies four quarter notes per measure and is sometimes designated with the symbol ¢ (for common time). The symbol ¢ stands for cut time (2/2). Most songs are either in 4/4 or 3/4.

TABLATURE

In tablature, the six horizontal lines represent the six strings of the guitar, with the first string on the top and sixth on the bottom. The numbers refer to fret numbers on a given string. The notation and tablature in this book are designed to be used in tandem—refer to the notation to get the rhythmic information and note durations, and refer to the tablature to get the exact locations of the notes on the guitar fingerboard.

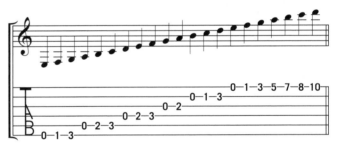

FINGERINGS

Fingerings are indicated with small numbers and letters in the notation. Fretting-hand fingering is indicated with 1 for the index finger, 2 the middle, 3 the ring, 4 the pinky, and *T* the thumb. Picking-hand fingering is indicated by *i* for the index finger, *m* the middle, *a* the ring, *c* the pinky, and *p* the thumb. Circled numbers indicate the string the note is played on. Remember that the fingerings indicated are only suggestions; if you find a different way that works better for you, use it.

PICK AND STRUM DIRECTION

In music played with a flatpick, downstrokes (toward the floor) and upstrokes (toward the ceiling) are shown as follows. Slashes in the notation and tablature indicate a strum through the previously played chord.

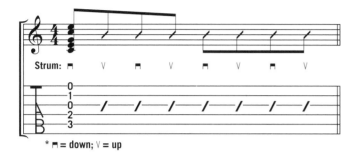

* ⊓ = down; V = up

CHORD DIAGRAMS

Chord diagrams show where the fingers go on the fingerboard. Frets are shown horizontally. The thick top line represents the nut. A Roman numeral to the right of a diagram indicates a chord played higher up the neck (in this case the top horizontal line is thin). Strings are shown as vertical lines. The line on the far left represents the sixth (lowest) string, and the line on the far right represents the first (highest) string. Dots show where the fingers go, and thick horizontal lines indicate barres. Numbers above the diagram are left-hand finger numbers, as used in standard notation. Again, the fingerings are only suggestions. An X indicates a string that should be muted or not played; 0 indicates an open string.

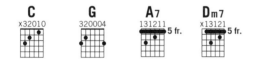

CAPOS

If a capo is used, a Roman numeral indicates the fret where the capo should be placed. The standard notation and tablature is written as if the capo were the nut of the guitar. For instance, a tune capoed anywhere up the neck and played using key-of-G chord shapes and fingerings will be written in the key of G. Likewise, open strings held down by the capo are written as open strings.

TUNINGS

Alternate guitar tunings are given from the lowest (sixth) string to the highest (first) string. For instance, D A D G B E indicates standard tuning with the bottom string dropped to D. Standard notation for songs in alternate tunings always reflects the actual pitches of the notes. Arrows underneath tuning notes indicate strings that are altered from standard tuning and whether they are tuned up or down.

VOCAL TUNES

Vocal tunes are sometimes written with a fully tabbed-out introduction and a vocal melody with chord diagrams for the rest of the piece. The tab intro is usually your indication of which strum or fingerpicking pattern to use in the rest of the piece. The melody with lyrics underneath is the melody sung by the vocalist. Occasionally, smaller notes are written with the melody to indicate the harmony part sung by another vocalist. These are not to be confused with cue notes, which are small notes that indicate melodies that vary when a section is repeated. Listen to a recording of the piece to get a feel for the guitar accompaniment and to hear the singing if you aren't skilled at reading vocal melodies.

ARTICULATIONS

There are a number of ways you can articulate a note on the guitar. Notes connected with slurs (not to be confused with ties) in the tablature or standard notation are articulated with either a hammer-on, pull-off, or slide. Lower notes slurred to higher notes are played as hammer-ons; higher notes slurred to lower notes are played as pull-offs. While it's usually obvious that slurred notes are played as hammer-ons or pull-offs, an H or P is included above the tablature as an extra reminder.

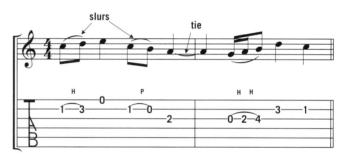

Slides are represented with a dash, and an S is included above the tab. A dash preceding a note represents a slide into the note from an indefinite point in the direction of the slide; a dash following a note indicates a slide off of the note to an indefinite point in the direction of the slide. For two slurred notes connected with a slide, you should pick the first note and then slide into the second.

Bends are represented with upward curves, as shown in the next example. Most bends have a specific destination pitch—the number above the bend symbol shows how much the bend raises the string's pitch: ¼ for a slight bend, ½ for a half step, 1 for a whole step.

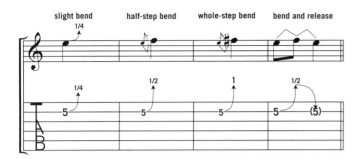

Grace notes are represented by small notes with a dash through the stem in standard notation and with small numbers in the tab. A grace note is a very quick ornament leading into a note, most commonly executed as a hammer-on, pull-off, or slide. In the following example, pluck the note at the fifth fret on the beat, then quickly hammer onto the seventh fret. The second example is executed as a quick pull-off from the second fret to the open string. In the third example, both notes at the fifth fret are played simultaneously (even though it appears that the fifth fret, fourth string, is to be played by itself), then the seventh fret, fourth string, is quickly hammered.

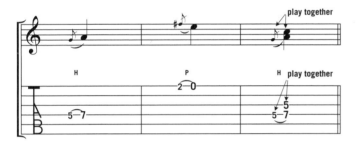

HARMONICS

Harmonics are represented by diamond-shaped notes in the standard notation and a small dot next to the tablature numbers. Natural harmonics are indicated with the text "Harmonics" or "Harm." above the tablature. Harmonics articulated with the right hand (often called artificial harmonics) include the text "R.H. Harmonics" or "R.H. Harm." above the tab. Right-hand harmonics are executed by lightly touching the harmonic node (usually 12 frets above the open string or fretted note) with the right-hand index finger and plucking the string with the thumb or ring finger or pick. For extended phrases played with right-hand harmonics, the fretted notes are shown in the tab along with instructions to touch the harmonics 12 frets above the notes.

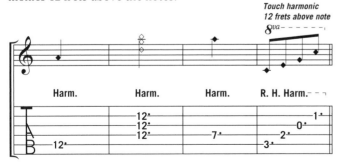

REPEATS

One of the most confusing parts of a musical score can be the navigation symbols, such as repeats, *D.S. al Coda, D.C. al Fine, To Coda,* etc.

Repeat symbols are placed at the beginning and end of the passage to be repeated.

You should ignore repeat symbols with the dots on the right side the first time you encounter them; when you come to a repeat symbol with dots on the left side, jump back to the previous repeat symbol facing the opposite direction (if there is no previous symbol, go to the beginning of the piece). The next time you come to the repeat symbol, ignore it and keep going unless it includes instructions such as "Repeat three times."

Often a section will have a different ending after each repeat. The example below includes a first and a second ending. Play until you hit the repeat symbol, jump back to the previous repeat symbol and play until you reach the bracketed first ending, skip the measures under the bracket and jump immediately to the second ending, and then continue.

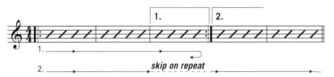

D.S. stands for *dal segno* or "from the sign." When you encounter this indication, jump immediately to the sign (𝄋). *D.S.* is usually accompanied by *al Fine* or *al Coda. Fine* indicates the end of a piece. *A coda* is a final passage near the end of a piece and is indicated with ⊕. *D.S. al Coda* simply tells you to jump back to the sign and continue on until you are instructed to jump to the coda, indicated with *To Coda* ⊕.

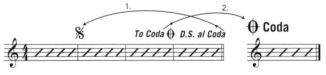

D.C. stands for *da capo* or "from the beginning." Jump to the top of the piece when you encounter this indication.

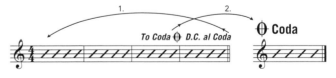

D.C. al Fine tells you to jump to the beginning of a tune and continue until you encounter the *Fine* indicating the end of the piece (ignore the *Fine* the first time through).

HAPPY AND YOU KNOW IT

This children's favorite is a great warm-up and activity song. You can easily improvise verses—try replacing "clap your hands" with "play guitar," for instance. The two quarter-rests in measure 2 indicate where to clap your hands! This is a simple three-chord progression sweetened with one additional chord. In the key of G, the Em in measure 6 nicely assists the G, C, and D7. Notice that the first two notes anticipate the first measure (or bar). These are also called pickup notes.

Since I was crazy about Elvis' "Hound Dog" when I was three years old, I get particular pleasure out of Little Richard's rockin' rendition of this tune on *Shake It All About* (Disney 60849). ✦

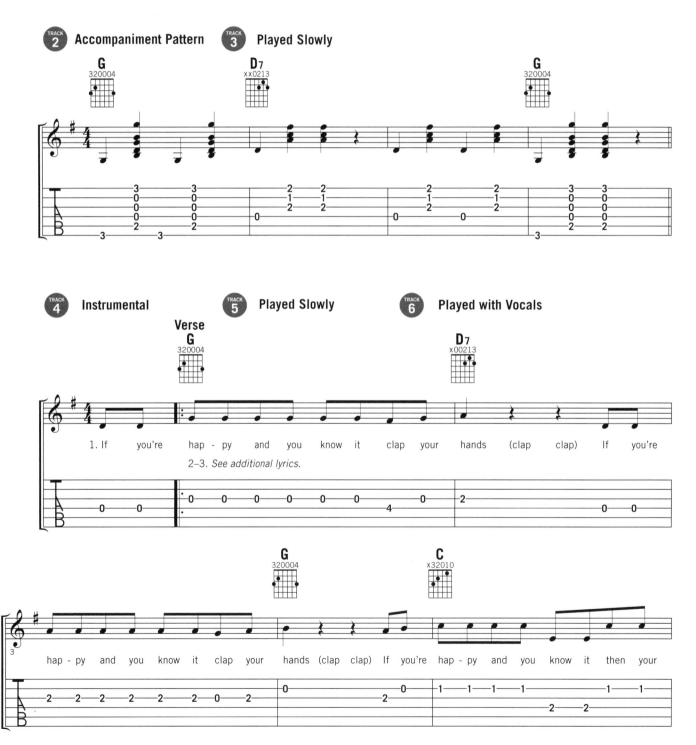

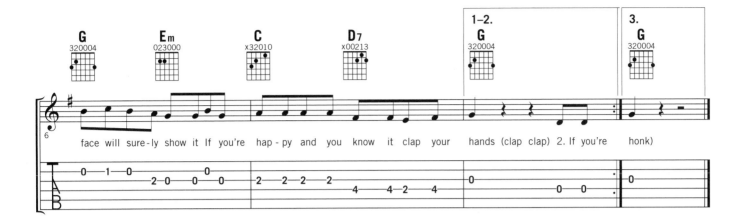

face will sure-ly show it If you're hap-py and you know it clap your hands (clap clap) 2. If you're honk)

<table>
<tr><td></td><td>G</td><td></td><td></td><td>D7</td></tr>
</table>

     G   D7

1.   If you're happy and you know it, clap your hands (clap, clap)

                                    G

If you're happy and you know it, clap your hands (clap, clap)

      C   G   Em

If you're happy and you know it, then your face will surely show it

      C   D7   G

If you're happy and you know it, clap your hands (clap, clap)

      G   D7

2.   If you're happy and you know it, stomp your feet (stomp, stomp)

                                    G

If you're happy and you know it, stomp your feet (stomp, stomp)

      C   G   Em

If you're happy and you know it, then your face will surely show it

      C   D7   G

If you're happy and you know it, stomp your feet (stomp, stomp)

      G   D7

3.   If you're happy and you know it, honk your nose (honk, honk)

                                    G

If you're happy and you know it, honk your nose (honk, honk)

      C   G   Em

If you're happy and you know it, then your face will surely show it

      C   D7   G

If you're happy and you know it, honk your nose (honk, honk)

BRAHMS' LULLABY

The quintessential lullaby was written by Johannes Brahms. The original first verse is from a German folk poem. The song uses a very simple three-chord progression in the key of G, and who doesn't have this melody indelibly in their soul? It's our first selection in 3/4 or waltz time, as most lullabies are. Once again, notice the two pickup notes prior to the first measure.

Good ol' singing cowboy Gene Autry does cowboy justice to the old master Brahms on *Gene Autry Sings Gene Autry and Other Favorites* (Essential Media Group). ◆

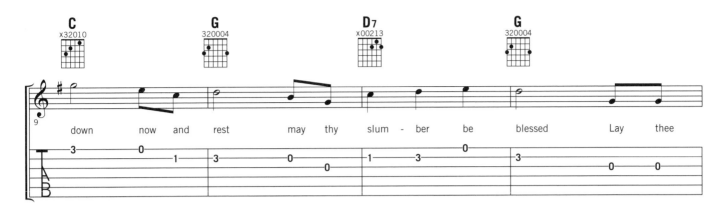

down   now   and   rest   may   thy   slum - ber   be   blessed   Lay   thee

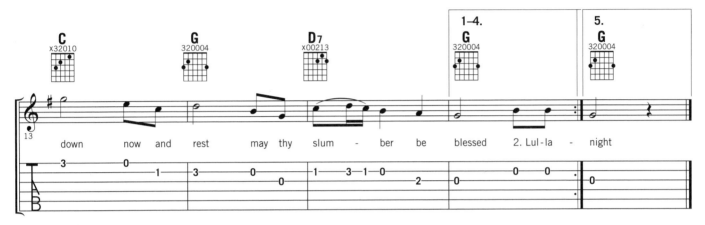

down   now   and   rest   may   thy   slum - ber   be   blessed   2. Lul - la - night

        G   D7

1. Lullaby and good night, with roses bedight

                               G

  With lilies o'er spread is baby's wee bed

      C   G   D7   G

  Lay thee down now and rest, may thy slumber be blessed

      C   G   D7   G

  Lay thee down now and rest, may thy slumber be blessed

        G   D7

2. Lullaby and good night, thy mother's delight

                               G

  Bright angels beside my darling abide

      C   G   D7   G

  They will guard thee at rest, thou shalt wake on my breast

      C   G   D7   G

  They will guard thee at rest, thou shalt wake on my breast

        G   D7

3. Sleepyhead, close your eyes, mother's right here beside you

                               G

  I'll protect you from harm, you will wake in my arms

      C   G   D7   G

  Guardian angels are near, so sleep on, with no fear

      C   G   D7   G

  Guardian angels are near, so sleep on, with no fear

        G   D7

4. Lullaby, and sleep tight, hush! My darling is sleeping

                               G

  On his sheets white as cream, with his head full of dreams

      C   G   D7   G

  When the sky's bright with dawn, he will wake in the morning

      C   G   D7   G

  When noontide warms the world, he will frolic in the sun

        G   D7

5. Go to sleep, little one, think of puppies and kittens

                               G

  Go to sleep, little one, think of butterflies in spring

      C   G   D7   G

  Go to sleep, little one, think of sunny bright mornings

      C   G   D7   G

  Go to sleep, little one, sleep tight through the night

MOCKINGBIRD

This traditional American lullaby can come in handy when the need arises to persuade a child to speak in a soft voice, as the lyrics suggest. It doesn't get much more simple: two chords, C and G..

Peter, Paul, and Mary give a very nice straightforward performance, complete with their sweetest folk harmonies, on *Peter, Paul, and Mommy* (Warner Bros. 2-1785). ✦

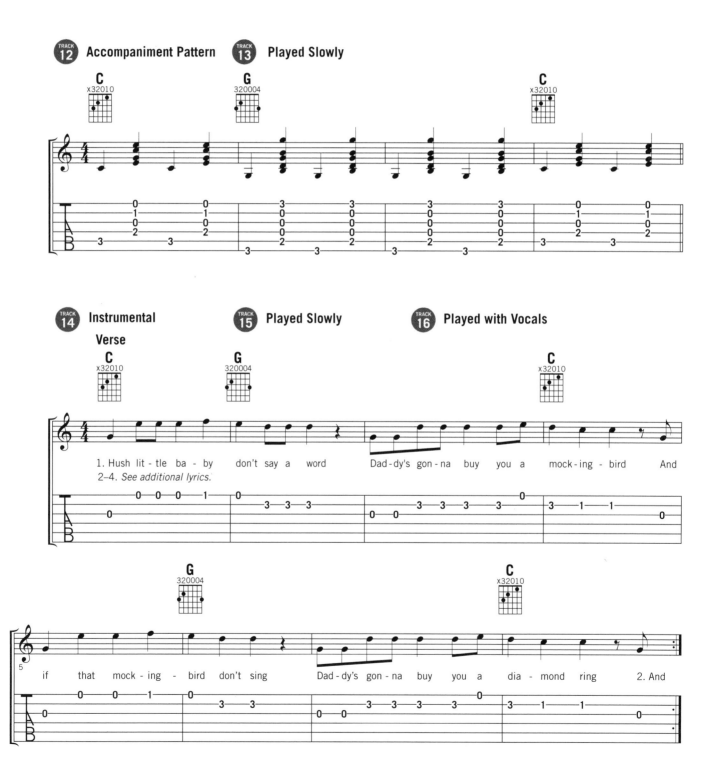

   C   G

1.   Hush, little baby, don't say a word

                 C

    Daddy's gonna buy you a mockingbird

            G

    And if that mockingbird don't sing

              C

    Daddy's gonna buy you a diamond ring

         C   G

2.   And if that diamond ring turn brass

             C

    Daddy's gonna buy you a looking glass

            G

    And if that looking glass gets broke

             C

    Daddy's gonna buy you a billy goat

        C   G

3.   And if that billy goat don't pull

              C

    Daddy's gonna buy you a cart and bull

            G

    And if that cart and bull turn over

             C

    Daddy's gonna buy you a dog named Rover

        C   G

4.   And if that dog named Rover won't bark

             C

    Daddy's gonna buy you a horse and cart

            G

    And if that horse and cart fall down

               C

    Well, you'll still be the sweetest little baby in town

GOLDEN SLUMBERS

The lyrics to this lullaby are from a poem by Elizabethan playwright Thomas Dekker, appearing first in his play "The Pleasant Comedy of Patient Grissill," somewhere around 1603. Paul McCartney put these words to his own music on the Beatles' final album, *Abbey Road*.

"Golden Slumbers" is in 3/4 time and is basically a three-chord progression, with the exception of the chord E7, which helps move the piece along smoothly and tastefully. Phil Rosenthal and Family perform this song with their authentic folk ensemble on *Folk Song Lullabies* (American Melody 5119).◆

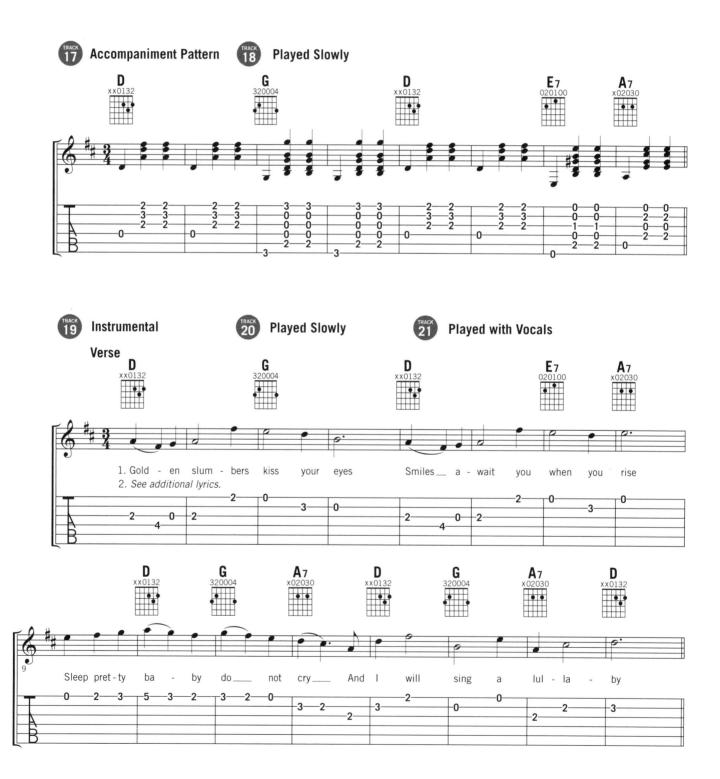

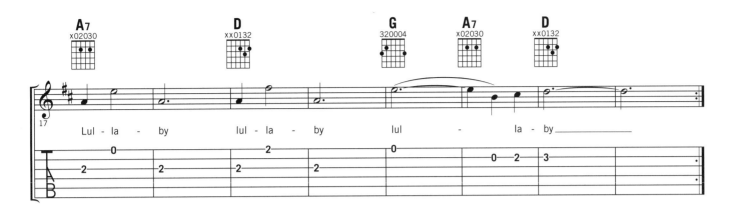

Lul - la - by   lul - la - by   lul - la - by _____

1. | D | | G |
   Golden slumbers kiss your eyes

   | D | | E7 | A7 |
   Smiles await you when you rise

   | | D | G | A7 |
   Sleep pretty baby do not cry

   | | D | G | A7 | G |
   And I will sing a lullaby

   | A7 | | D | | G A7 D |
   Lullaby, lullaby, lullaby

2. | D | | G |
   Cares you know not, therefore sleep

   | D | | E7 | A7 |
   While over you, a watch I'll keep

   | | D | G | A7 |
   Sleep pretty darling do not cry

   | | D | G | A7 | G |
   And I will sing a lullaby

   | A7 | | D | | G A7 D |
   Lullaby, lullaby, lullaby

SHOO FLY

For a long time we have been saying "shoo, fly!" . . . and singing it too! The song was written in the 1860s by Billy Reeves (words) and Frank Campbell (music).

"Shoo Fly" is in the key of D and in 4/4 time with a swing feel, and uses just two chords, D and A7. One slightly tricky aspect: notice that several of the chords change in the middle rather than in the beginning of a measure (e.g., measures 2, 4, and 6). Also, the melody stretches to the fifth fret in measure 7, so you'll have to use your pinky to make this stretch!

The legendary Pete Seeger delivers a lively a cappella rendition on *American Folk, Game, and Activity Songs for Children* (Smithsonian Folkways 45056). ◆

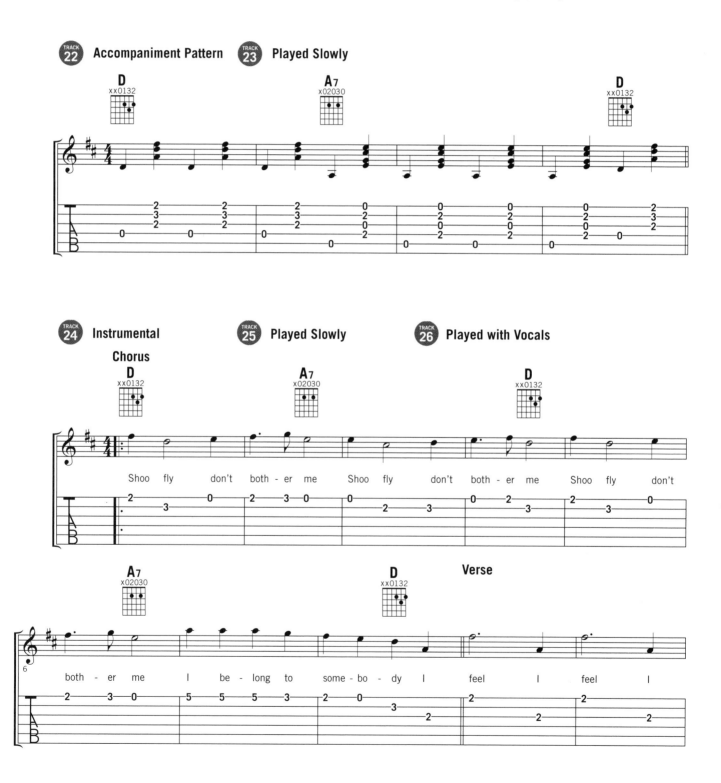

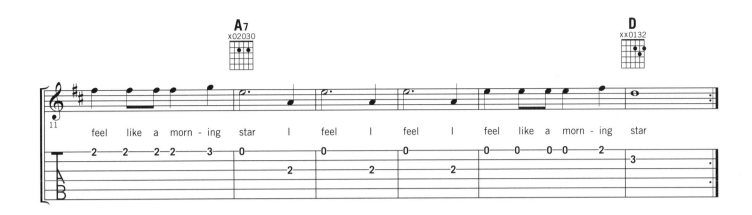

feel like a morn - ing star I feel I feel I feel like a morn - ing star

Chorus

D   **A7**
Shoo, fly, don't bother me

                    D
Shoo, fly, don't bother me

                    A7
Shoo, fly, don't bother me

                    D
For I belong to somebody

D
1. I feel, I feel

                                    A7
    I feel like a morning star

    I feel, I feel

                                    D
    I feel like a morning star

MY BONNIE LIES OVER THE OCEAN

This is a traditional Scottish folk song. The Beatles covered "Bonnie" with rock 'n' roll verve, backing up Tony Sheridan, on one of their earliest recordings. This song is in the key of D and in 3/4 time; notice the lone pickup note. The verse uses a three-chord progression (D, G, A7), with the additional help of E7. We can then relax in the chorus as it uses the easy three chords only.

The Sons of the Pioneers bestow their plaintive cowboy harmonies on us on *Songs of the Prairie* (Bear Family 15710). ✦

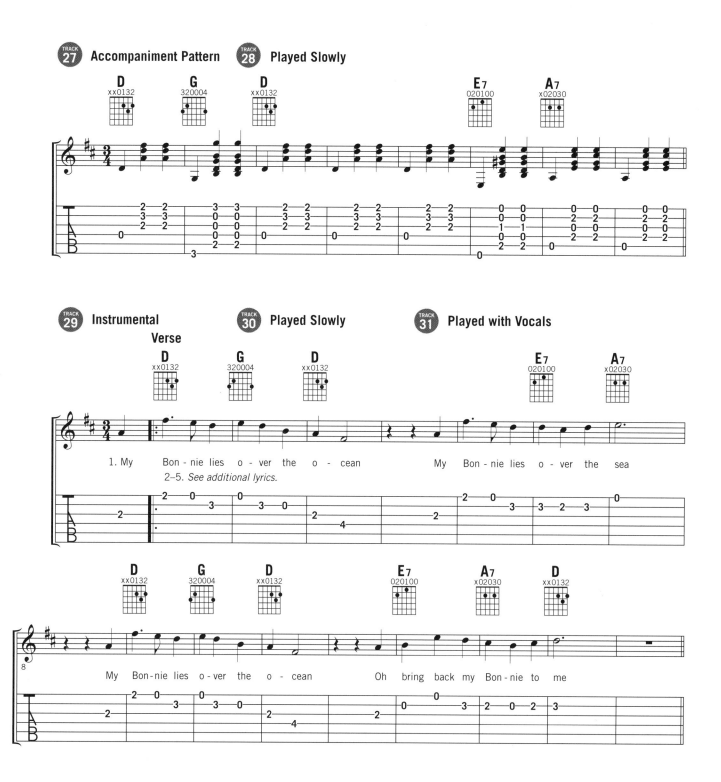

Chorus

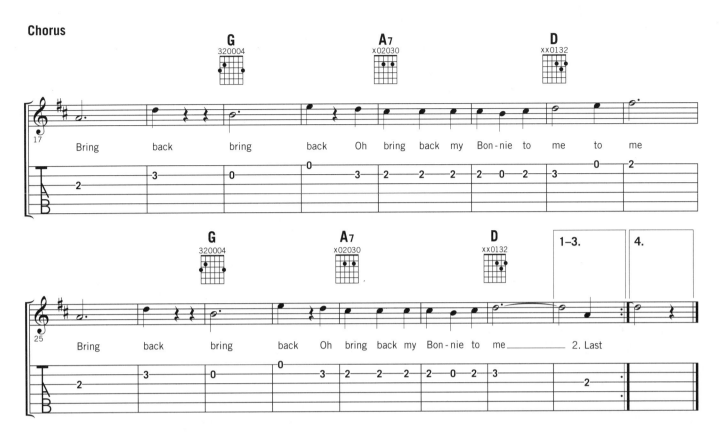

1.   **D**   **G**   **D**
    My Bonnie lies over the ocean

              E7   **A7**
    My Bonnie lies over the sea

    D   **G**   **D**
    My Bonnie lies over the ocean

    G   **A7**   **D**
    Oh bring back my Bonnie to me

    Chorus

    D   **G**
    Bring back, bring back

    A7   **D**
    Oh bring back my Bonnie to me, to me

    G
    Bring back, bring back

    A7   **D**
    Oh, bring back my Bonnie to me

2.   **D**   **G**   **D**
    Last night as I lay on my pillow

              E7   **A7**
    Last night as I lay on my bed

    D   **G**   **D**
    Last night as I lay on my pillow

    G   **A7**   **D**
    I dreamed that my Bonnie was dead

Repeat Chorus

3.   **D**   **G**   **D**
    Oh blow ye the winds o'er the ocean

              E7   **A7**
    And blow ye the winds o'er the sea

    D   **G**   **D**
    Oh blow ye the winds o'er the ocean

    G   **A7**   **D**
    And bring back my Bonnie to me

Repeat Chorus

4.   **D**   **G**   **D**
    The winds have blown over the ocean

              E7   **A7**
    The winds have blown over the sea

    D   **G**   **D**
    The winds have blown over the ocean

    G   **A7**   **D**
    And brought back my Bonnie to me

Repeat Chorus

MAKE NEW FRIENDS

This traditional ditty has been sung around many a campfire. Its message is pure: "Make new friends, but keep the old / One is silver and the other gold."

This song has a simple three-chord progression in A, in 4/4 time, and works great as a round! Cathy Fink and Marcy Marxer lead a nice sing-along (with some mean conga-drum playing!) on *Cathy and Marcy's Song Shop* DVD (Community). ✦

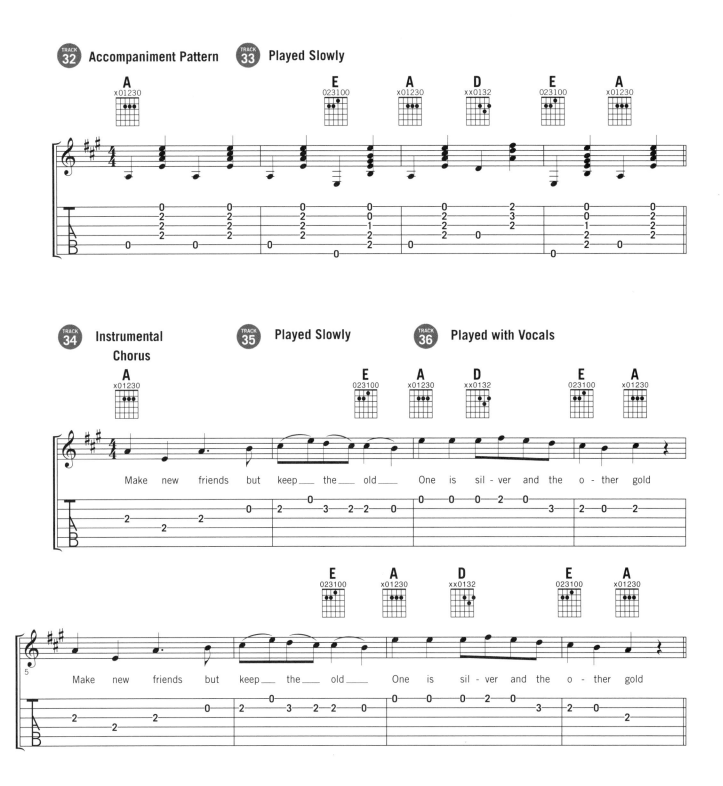

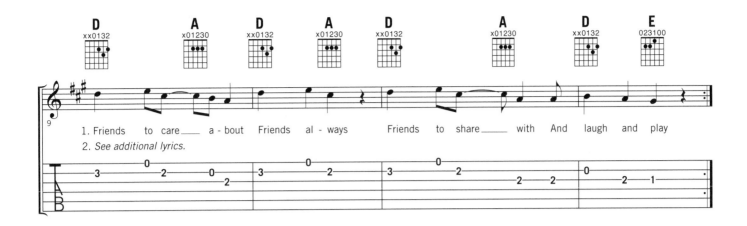

Chorus

A   **E**
Make new friends, but keep the old

A **D**   **E** **A**
One is silver and the other gold

A   **E**
Make new friends, but keep the old

A **D**   **E** **A**
One is silver and the other gold

  D   **A**
1. Friends to care about

  D **A**
 Friends always

  D   **A**
 Friends to share with

   D **E**
 And laugh and play

Repeat Chorus

  D   **A**
2. Friends to trust with

  D **A**
 Friends to love

  D   **A**
 Friends to talk with

   D **E**
 And friends to hug

Repeat Chorus

THE BEAR WENT OVER THE MOUNTAIN

Sung to the tune of "For He's a Jolly Good Fellow" (the words of which are also included here), what better song for making one feel happy and special! We are in the key of E and in 3/4 time, with E, E7, A, and my old friend, the fabulous B7! Notice the pickup and don't forget the fermata (or bird's eye) in measures 12 and 28, which indicates that you

hold a note for a bit—you know, "the bear went over the mountaaaaiiiinnnn . . ."

Sesame Street's Bob McGrath, who has been nurturing baby's hearts for 40 years, includes this song on *Sing Along with Bob, Vol. 1* (Bob's Kids 4100903).   ◆

1.
    E   A E
    The bear went over the mountain

    B7   E
    The bear went over the mountain

                   A
    The bear went over the mountain

    E B7   E
    To see what he could see

         A   E
    To see what he could see

         A   E
    To see what he could see

        E7   A
    The bear went over the mountain

    B7   E
    To see what he could see

2.
    E   A E
    For he's a jolly good fellow

    B7   E
    For he's a jolly good fellow

               A
    For he's a jolly good fellow

    E B7   E
    Which nobody can deny

         A   E
    Which nobody can deny

         A   E
    Which nobody can deny

        E7   A
    For he's a jolly good fellow

    B7   E
    Which nobody can deny

THIS OLD MAN

Easily one of the all-time favorite children's songs, and certainly one of the first that I ever learned to sing. Everybody knows it. Such a happy and fun song—also a great counting song, of course. There are many versions; one source is Anne Gilcrest, who learned it from her Welsh nurse in the 1870s. How fortunate we are that wonderful music is kept alive by being passed on from generation to generation.

Though a simple two-chord progression in C, using just C and G7, "This Old Man" has that fifth-fret stretch in bar 3. Just use that little pinky finger!

Pete Seeger sings "This Old Man" on *American Folk, Game, and Activity Songs for Children* (Smithsonian Folkways 45056). ◆

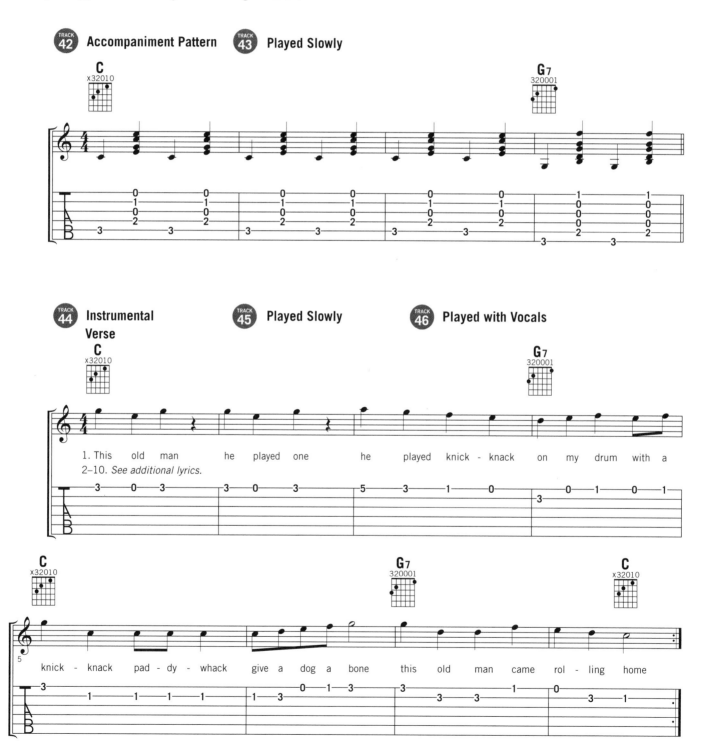

```
     C
1.   This old man, he played one
                       G7
     He played knick-knack on my drum
                C
     With a knick-knack, paddy whack give a dog a bone
     G7               C
     This old man came rolling home


     C
2.   This old man, he played two
                       G7
     He played knick-knack on my shoe
                C
     With a knick-knack, paddy whack give a dog a bone
     G7               C
     This old man came rolling home


     C
3.   This old man, he played three
                       G7
     He played knick-knack on my knee
                C
     With a knick-knack, paddy whack give a dog a bone
     G7               C
     This old man came rolling home


     C
4.   This old man, he played four
                       G7
     He played knick-knack on the floor
                C
     With a knick-knack, paddy whack give a dog a bone
     G7               C
     This old man came rolling home


     C
5.   This old man, he played five
                       G7
     He played knick-knack on my knife
                C
     With a knick-knack, paddy whack give a dog a bone
     G7               C
     This old man came rolling home
```

```
     C
6.   This old man, he played six
                       G7
     He played knick-knack with some sticks
                C
     With a knick-knack, paddy whack give a dog a bone
     G7               C
     This old man came rolling home


     C
7.   This old man, he played seven
                       G7
     He played knick-knack up in heaven
                C
     With a knick-knack, paddy whack give a dog a bone
     G7               C
     This old man came rolling home


     C
8.   This old man, he played eight
                       G7
     He played knick-knack on my gate
                C
     With a knick-knack, paddy whack give a dog a bone
     G7               C
     This old man came rolling home


     C
9.   This old man, he played nine
                       G7
     He played knick-knack on my spine
                C
     With a knick-knack, paddy whack give a dog a bone
     G7               C
     This old man came rolling home


     C
10.  This old man, he played ten
                       G7
     He played knick-knack on my shin
                C
     With a knick-knack, paddy whack give a dog a bone
     G7               C
     This old man came rolling home
```

THE MORE WE GET TOGETHER

Sung to the tune of "Did You Ever See a Lassie," this is a two-chord waltz in A. As practice makes perfect, we get the chords together, the time together, the waltz feel together, the "playing together" together . . . the more we get together, the happier we'll be!

This song can be heard on *I Love to Sing with Barney* (Koch 8616). While working with babies, I noticed this cute peculiarity: up until the age of three they always want to hear Barney. When they are about three and a half, you say, "Would you like to hear Barney?" and they say, "Nooo!"   ◆

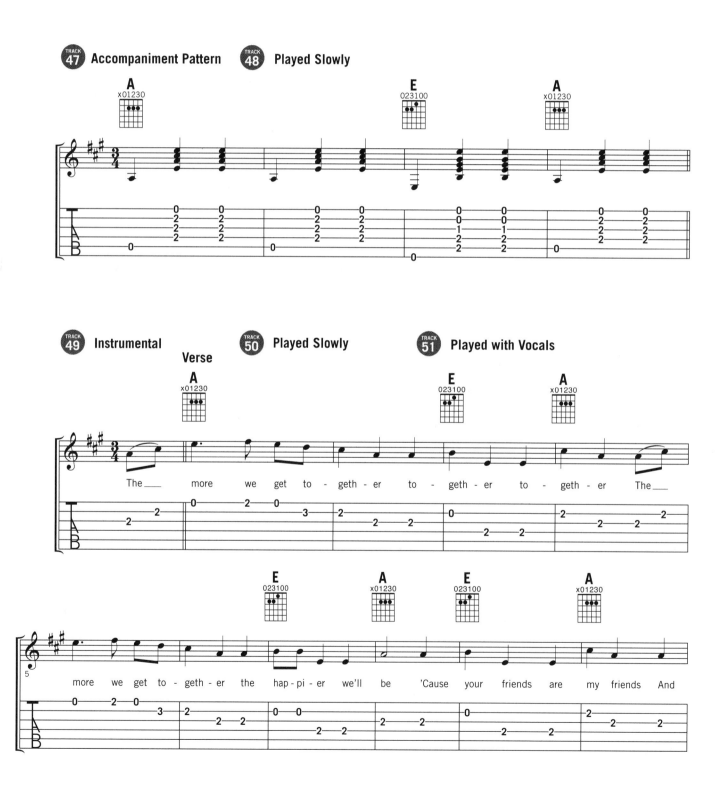

my friends are your friends The ___ more we get to - geth - er the hap - pi - er we'll be

1.   The more we get together, together, together
         (A)   (E) (A)

    The more we get together, the happier we'll be
                   (E)   (A)

    'Cause your friends are my friends and my friends are your friends
      (E)   (A)   (E)   (A)

    The more we get together, the happier we'll be
                   (E)   (A)

KOOKABURRA

Kids love animal songs, and this one is unique. The kookaburra is a very large bird native to Australia and New Guinea. Kookaburras are known for their call, which sounds like a human laughing loudly. The song is in 4/4 and the key of G, with a slightly different yet equally effective two-chord progression. Rather than the expected G to D, "Kookaburra" goes from G to C. This one also works great as a round!

Wendy Wiseman puts a modern twist on this classic from down under on *Top 30 Toddler Songs* (Kidzup 010517). ◆

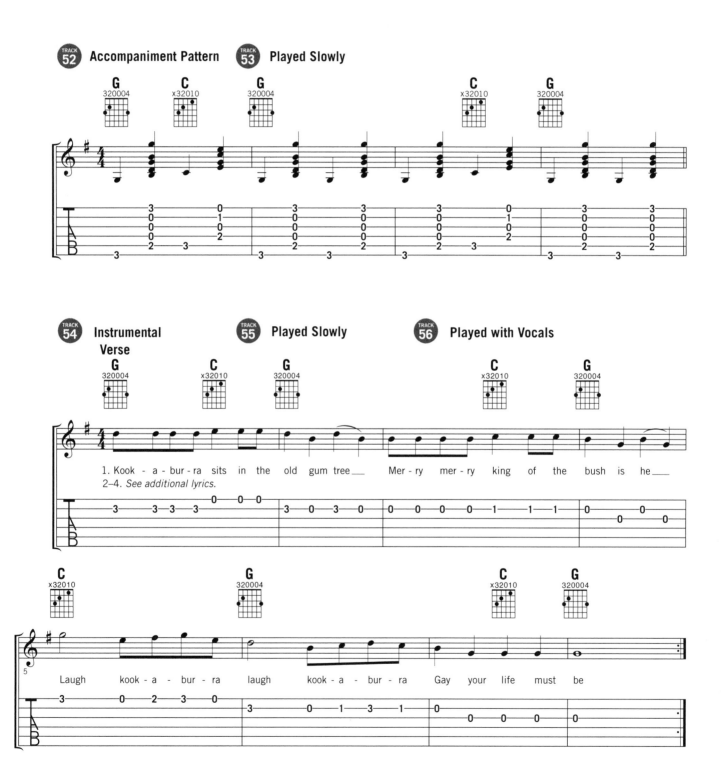

```
     G             C              G
1.   Kookaburra sits in the old gum tree
                   C              G
     Merry, merry king of the bush is he
     C                        G
     Laugh, kookaburra! Laugh, kookaburra!
                   C        G
     Gay your life must be


     G             C              G
2.   Kookaburra sits in the old gum tree
                   C              G
     Eating all the gum drops he can see
     C                    G
     Stop, kookaburra! Stop, kookaburra!
                   C        G
     Leave some there for me
```

```
     G             C              G
3.   Kookaburra sits in the old gum tree
                       C          G
     Counting all the monkeys he can see
     C                          G
     Stop, kookaburra! Stop, kookaburra!
                   C          G
     That's not a monkey, that's me


     G             C          G
4.   Kookaburra sits on a rusty nail
                   C          G
     Gets a boo-boo in his tail
     C                    G
     Cry, kookaburra! Cry, kookaburra!
                   C        G
     Oh how life can be
```

DOWN IN THE VALLEY

This is one of the very first songs I ever learned as an aspiring nine-year-old guitarist. Even though it's in a major key and the lyrics are basically positive, the song has kind of a melancholy effect. It's in the key of D and in 3/4 time, and uses just two chords (D and A7), but this arrangement has the added layer of using three-measure phrases, as you can see in the accompaniment pattern. You might find this a little tricky at first, but it has a natural circular flow.

The man in black, Johnny Cash, lends his inimitable basso pathos to "Down in the Valley" on disc three of *The Legend* (Columbia/Legacy 92802). ✦

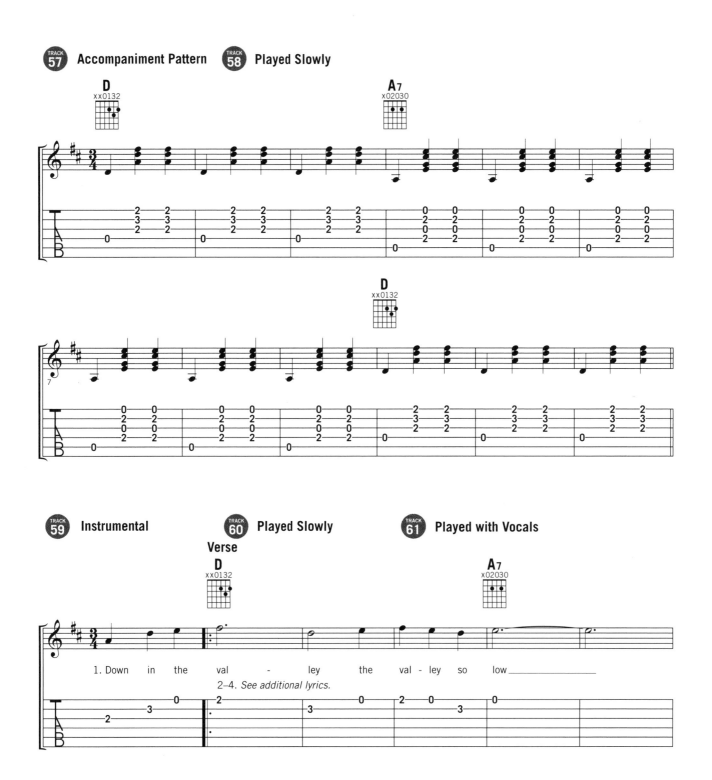

D
xx0132

Hang your head o - ver hear the wind blow_____

A7
x02030

Hear the wind blow dear hear the wind blow_____ Hang your head

D
xx0132

o - ver hear the wind blow_____ 2. Ros-es love

	D	A7
1.	Down in the valley, the valley so low	

                            D
Hang your head over, hear the wind blow

                                  A7
Hear the wind blow, dear, hear the wind blow

                            D
Hang your head over, hear the wind blow

	D	A7
2.	Roses love sunshine, violets love dew	

                            D
Angels in heaven know I love you

                            A7
Know I love you, dear, know I love you

                            D
Angels in heaven know I love you

	D	A7
3.	Writing this letter, containing three lines	

                            D
Answer my question, "Will you be mine?

                              A7
Will you be mine, dear, will you be mine?"

                            D
Answer my question, "Will you be mine?"

	D	A7
4.	Down in the valley, the valley so low	

                            D
Hang your head over, hear the wind blow

                              A7
Hear the wind blow, dear, hear the wind blow

                            D
Hang your head over, hear the wind blow

OVER IN THE MEADOW

This song has a couple of things going for it. Not only is it an animal song, but it has a bunch of animals in it! And, like "This Old Man," it's also a counting song. The main four-chord progression, using the chords G, Em, Am7 and D7, is slightly more complex than other songs in this book. There's one little quick chord change in measure 4, Am7 to D7 to G (see the accompaniment pattern). This will become natural with practice. Measures 5 and 6 use just G and C a couple of times, so you get a break, then it's off to the finish with the four-chord progression once again for the last two bars.

Kids' favorite Raffi makes lots of fun animal noises in his playful rendition on *Animal Songs* (Rounder 618145). ✦

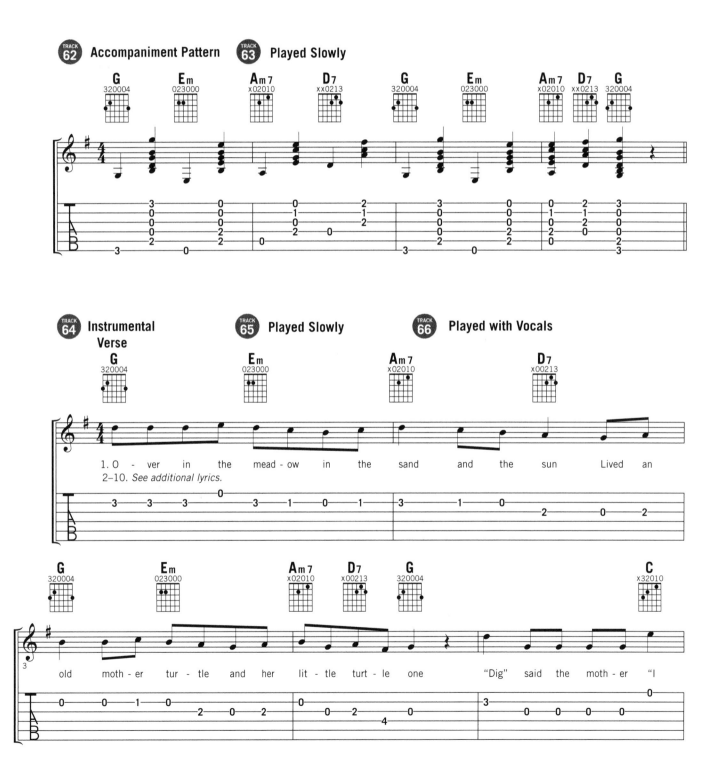

Chord diagrams: G (320004), C (x32010), G (320004), Em (023000), Am7 (x02010), D7 (x00213), G (320004)

Tab lyrics under staff: dig" said the one And they dug all____ day____ in the sand in the sun

G Em Am7 D7		**G** Em Am7 D7	

1. Over in the meadow in the sand in the sun

        G   **Em**   **Am7 D7** **G**
Lived an old mother turtle and her little turtle one

        C G
"Dig," said the mother, "I dig," said the one

C   **G**   **Em**   **Am7 D7**   **G**
And they dug all day in the sand in the sun

    G   **Em**   **Am7**   **D7**
2. Over in the meadow where the stream runs blue

        G   **Em**   **Am7 D7** **G**
Lived an old mother fish and her little fishies two

        C G
"Swim," said the mother, "We swim," said the two

C   **G**   **Em**   **Am7 D7 G**
And they swam all day where the stream runs blue

    G   **Em**   **Am7**   **D7**
3. Over in the meadow in a hole in the tree

        G   **Em**   **Am7 D7** **G**
Lived an old mother owl and her little owls three

        C G
"Whoo," said the mother, "We whoo," said the three

C   **G**   **Em**   **Am7 D7** **G**
And they whooed all day in the hole in the tree

    G   **Em**   **Am7**   **D7**
4. Over in the meadow by the old barn door

        G   **Em**   **Am7 D7** **G**
Lived an old mother rat and her little ratties four

        C G
"Gnaw," said the mother, "We gnaw," said the four

C   **G**   **Em**   **Am7 D7** **G**
And they gnawed all day by the old barn door

    G   **Em**   **Am7**   **D7**
5. Over in the meadow in a snug beehive

        G   **Em**   **Am7 D7** **G**
Lived an old mother bee and her little bees five

        C G
"Buzz," said the mother, "We buzz," said the five

C   **G**   **Em**   **Am7 D7 G**
And they buzzed all day in the snug beehive

    G   **Em**   **Am7**   **D7**
6. Over in the meadow in a nest built of sticks

        G   **Em**   **Am7 D7** **G**
Lived an old mother crow and her little crows six

        C G
"Caw," said the mother, "We caw," said the six

C   **G**   **Em**   **Am7 D7** **G**
And they cawed all day in the nest built of sticks

    G   **Em**   **Am7**   **D7**
7. Over in the meadow where the grass grows so even

        G   **Em**   **Am7 D7** **G**
Lived an old mother frog and her little froggies seven

        C G
"Jump," said the mother "We jump," said the seven

C   **G**   **Em**   **Am7 D7** **G**
And they jumped all day where the grass grows so even

    G   **Em**   **Am7**   **D7**
8. Over in the meadow by the old mossy gate

        G   **Em**   **Am7 D7** **G**
Lived an old mother lizard and her little lizards eight

        C G
"Bask," said the mother "We bask," said the eight

C   **G**   **Em**   **Am7 D7** **G**
And they basked all day by the old mossy gate

    G   **Em**   **Am7**   **D7**
9. Over in the meadow by the old scotch pine

        G   **Em**   **Am7 D7** **G**
Lived an old mother duck and her little duckies nine

        C G
"Quack," said the mother "We quack," said the nine

C   **G**   **Em**   **Am7 D7** **G**
And they quacked all day by the old scotch pine

    G   **Em**   **Am7**   **D7**
10. Over in the meadow in a cozy, wee den

        G   **Em**   **Am7 D7** **G**
Lived an old mother beaver and her little beavers ten

        C G
"Beave," said the mother "We beave," said the ten

C   **G**   **Em**   **Am7 D7 G**
And they beaved all day in their cozy wee den

ALL THE PRETTY LITTLE HORSES

This beautiful lullaby was sung by slaves to their masters before the Civil War. The lyric "wee little lamby . . . cried for her mammy" alludes to the pain of separation from their families that the slaves felt while being forced to work on the plantations. The great folklorist Alan Lomax learned it from his own mother in North Carolina and introduced it into the mainstream in the early 20th century.

This song is in a minor key (A minor), which takes nothing away from its beauty or ability to lull. It's also a bit complex, but demystifiable. The C in the verse enhances the movement of the three-chord progression Am–Dm–E7. In a beautiful twist, the bridge offers a glimmer of sunshine, as the songs shifts into the key of C major (A minor is called the relative minor of C major). There's one little pinky stretch to the fifth fret in fourth-to-last measure.

Give a listen to Joan Baez' beautiful and haunting rendition on *Baptism* (Vanguard 79275). ✦

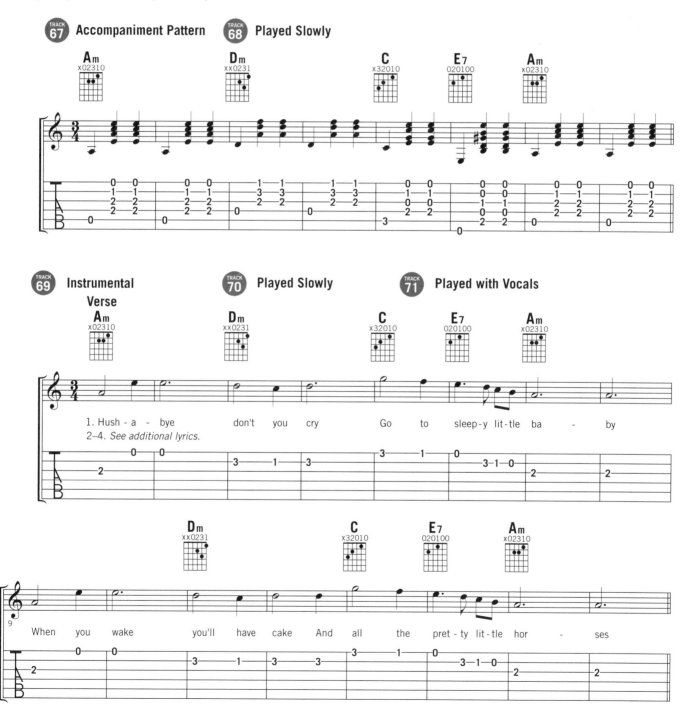

Chorus

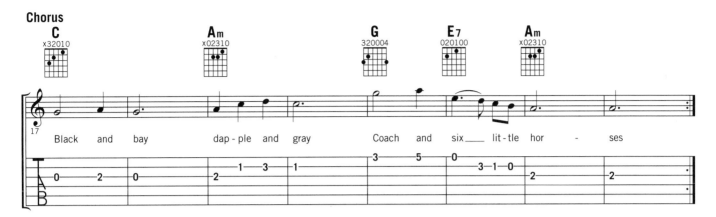

Black   and   bay   dap-ple   and   gray   Coach   and   six___   lit-tle   hor   -   ses

1.

Am   Dm
Hush-a-bye, don't you cry

C   E7   Am
Go to sleepy little baby

Dm
When you wake, you'll have cake

C   E7   Am
And all the pretty little horses

Chorus

C   Am
Black and bay, dapple and gray

G   E7   Am
Coach and six little horses

2.

Am   Dm
Way down yonder, in the meadow

C   E7   Am
There's a poor wee little lamby

Dm
The birds and the butterflies flutter 'round its eyes

C   E7   Am
The poor wee thing cried for her mammy

Repeat Chorus

3.

Am   Dm
Hush-a-bye, don't you cry

C   E7   Am
Go to sleepy little baby

Dm
When you wake, you'll have cake

C   E7   Am
And all the pretty little horses

Repeat Chorus

4.

Am   Dm
Hush-a-bye, don't you cry

C   E7   Am
Go to sleepy little baby

Dm
When you wake, you'll have cake

C   E7   Am
And all the pretty little horses

JENNY JENKINS

This traditional and oh-so-fun American tune is attributed to many sources. Among these, John and Alan Lomax learned it from Mr. and Mrs. E.C. Ball of Virginia in 1937. "Jenny Jenkins" uses an easy three-chord progression in the key of A and is in 4/4 time. The only slight oddity is the nonsense wordplay that extends over bars 7–10. That's not typical in terms of number of bars, but fun and not uncommon for this type of music. Hey, rules were made to be broken! And Mom and Dad can sing this as a duet!

Jerry Garcia and David Grisman's playful and dawg-gone old-timey arrangement of "Jenny Jenkins" is a must-listen (*Not for Kids Only*, Acoustic Disc 9). ◆

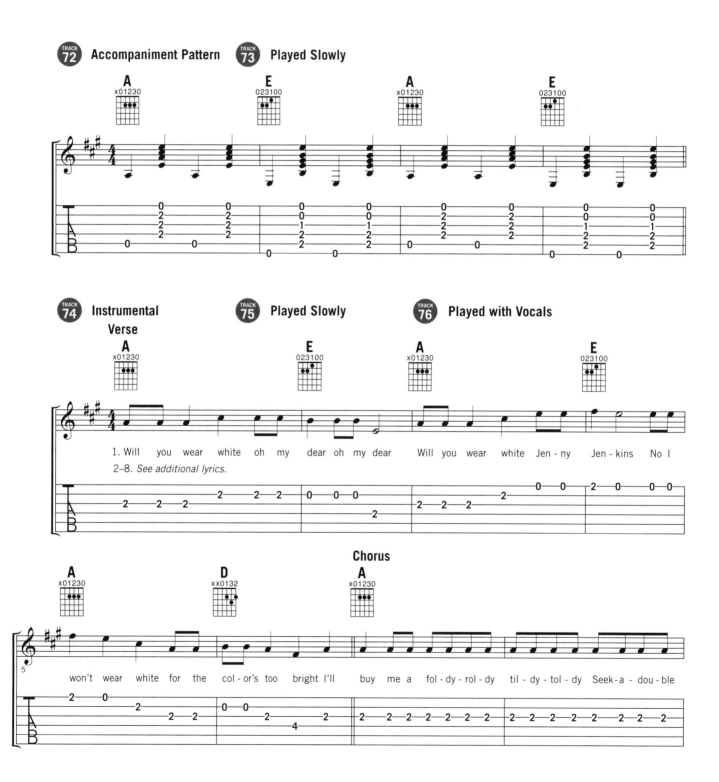

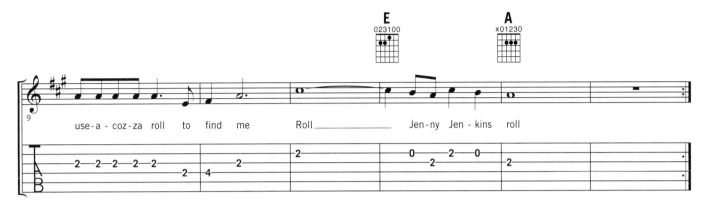

use-a-coz-za roll to find me   Roll_____ Jen-ny Jen-kins roll

A   **E**
1. Will you wear white oh my dear, oh my dear

    A   **E**
    Will you wear white, Jenny Jenkins?

        A   **D**
    No, I won't wear white for the color's too bright

    Chorus

        A
    I'll buy me a foldy-roldy, tildy-toldy

    Seek-a-double, use-a-cozza roll to find me

        E   **A**
    Roll, Jenny Jenkins, roll

    A   **E**
2. Will you wear green oh my dear, oh my dear

    A   **E**
    Will you wear green, Jenny Jenkins?

        A   **D**
    No, I won't wear green, it's a shame to be seen

    Repeat Chorus

    A   **E**
3. Will you wear blue oh my dear, oh my dear

    A   **E**
    Will you wear blue, Jenny Jenkins?

        A   **D**
    No, I won't wear blue for the color's too true

    Repeat Chorus

    A   **E**
4. Will you wear yellow oh my dear, oh my dear

    A   **E**
    Will you wear yellow, Jenny Jenkins?

        A   **D**
    No, I won't wear yellow for I'd never get a fellow

Repeat Chorus

    A   **E**
5. Will you wear brown oh my dear, oh my dear

    A   **E**
    Will you wear brown, Jenny Jenkins?

        A   **D**
    No, I won't wear brown for I'd never get around

    Repeat Chorus

    A   **E**
6. Will you wear beige oh my dear, oh my dear

    A   **E**
    Will you wear beige, Jenny Jenkins?

        A   **D**
    No I won't wear beige for it shows my age

    Repeat Chorus

    A   **E**
7. Will you wear orange oh my dear, oh my dear

    A   **E**
    Will you wear orange, Jenny Jenkins?

        A   **D**
    No, orange I won't wear, and it rhymes, so there

    Repeat Chorus

    A   **E**
8. What will you wear oh my dear, oh my dear

    A   **E**
    What will you wear, Jenny Jenkins?

        A   **D**
    Oh what do you care if I just go bare?

    Repeat Chorus

ABOUT THE AUTHOR

Peter Penhallow began playing piano and imitating Elvis Presley at the age of three, and he took up guitar at age nine. When he is not writing songs, accompanying singers, or jamming with friends, he enjoys recording music. Penhallow has been a musical director for children's and community musical theater in Marin County, California, for 30 years, and has more than 100 productions to his credit. He has also been an accompanist for Music Makers of Marin, a music school for preschool–aged children, for 20 years. Penhallow is currently the bandleader for the Liddypudlians, a Beatles tribute band with full orchestra. He has five CDs for young children to his credit, and he is the author of *Christmas Songs for Beginning Guitar*, *Children's Songs for Beginning Guitar*, and *Traditional Songs for Beginning Guitar* (String Letter Publishing).

Get More from Your Guitar

LEARN NEW SONGS, TECHNIQUES, AND MORE.

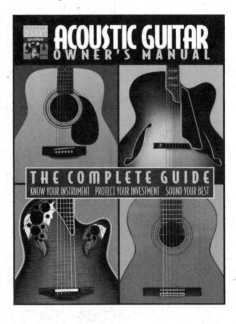

Acoustic Rock Essentials

Learn to play like your favorite acoustic rockstars. Andrew DuBrock returns with this follow up to his best-selling title, *Acoustic Rock Basics*. You will not be dissapointed.

Acoustic Guitar Owner's Manual

Understand your instruments and preserve and protect their value.

"Guitar junkies and novices alike will find much interesting and useful information in this book."
—*Wood & Steel*

Also Available

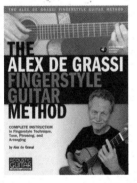

The Alex de Grassi Fingerstyle Guitar Method

A complete course in contemporary steel-string guitar.

Weekly Workout

Daily excercises to improve your guitar technique.

Irish Songs for Guitar

Danny Carnahan's 15 favorite Irish songs arranged for acoustic guitar.

Acoustic Rock Basics

Andrew DuBrock teaches basics of acoustic rock guitar.

Fingerstyle Jazz Guitar Essentials

Learn the art of fingerstyle jazz guitar with Sean McGowan.

Acoustic Guitar Amplification Essentials

The ultimate guide to amplifying your acoustic guitar.

Carter-Style Guitar Basics

Learn the boom-chuck rhythm, pioneered by Maybelle Carter.

Spanish Repertoire for Classical Guitar

Learn Spanish classical pieces from Francisco Tárrega, Julian Arcas, and more.

The Acoustic Guitar Method

Based on traditional American music, this book teaches you authentic techniques and songs.

Holiday Songs for Fingerstyle Guitar

Unique fingerstyle arrangements of classic holiday songs.